Reality Stain

Reality Stain
by Ziad Dib Jreige
Paperback Edition

First Published in 2023 by

Inkfeathers Publishing
Vivek Vihar, New Delhi 110095
www.inkfeathers.com

ISBN 978-81-19483-11-2

Review for "The Nightingale" by Ziad Dib Jreige

Zandra
United Kingdom | January 2, 2022

I have been a supporter of the Lebanese poet Ziad Dib Jreige since coming across his poetry on Instagram some two years ago. His poetry blends precise observations of nature with spiritual awareness gained primarily through his own immediate natural world.

Our poet skilfully connects humankind as part of nature and through his rhythm creating a richness of imagery. He seamlessly marries the two, with his own lyrical grace and beauty.

He is an accomplished contemporary, reminiscent at times of those quintessential romantic era poets. I sense his expressions of care and depth of emotion throughout each of his poems.

He is unafraid to explore other cultures and languages he has learned and loved, delicately crafting his poetry with intellect, wisdom, spirituality, philosophy, and scientific analyses of nature and life experience.

He describes himself as a nightingale in his own dawn. singing of love, joy, doubt, reflection, loss and agony. Presenting us with a reading triumph. Possessing sharp awareness to develop exquisite tone, and the ability to create a mesmerising atmosphere. Frequently moving one to tears.

His affinity for solitude and inner monologues offer a tender insight. The influences that inspire him, that sense of wonder so deeply instilled shines through, which is generously bestowed in every aspect of life through his creative lens.

The Nightingale by Ziad Dib Jreige was a pure joy to read, and shall remain in my collection. I am delighted to recommend, and award a well-deserved five stars.

Reality Stain

Ziad Dib Jreige

Inkfeathers Publishing
www.inkfeathers.com

This book is dedicated with much gratefulness
to my mother Kamal Abdel Massih.
As well as to my love Dzovig Arnelian.

Dear mom,

I would have turned into a good doctor to help
thousands, but my words will help millions.
Thank you for the immeasurable support.

Dear Dzovig,

I understand all the messed up relationships
I'd been through before I met you.
They all make perfect sense now.

Thank you for the immeasurable trust.

Poet's Note

The ability for a human to understand and analyse is exponential. The vast universe will soon be our playground, nevertheless things as small as a seed will always make us wonder and wander.

Books form a reliable bridge, to that parallel universe, in which we can escape the many bars put around our bodies, minds and souls. A universe that we can surely reach with movies, songs, paintings, and other forms of art. Reading is one of the most impactful ways of travel to and from that world. Sometimes a house of childhood, sometimes an eldercare home, and sometimes a trip with unusual senses and unfamiliar abilities.

In a time of fast paced operations, stress has led many to drift away from themselves, away from where they should be. The inner peace is less and less common among individuals. The societies seem to regularly upgrade their requirements, putting more and more pressure on people to give them the "label" of belonging. My quest to understand more about myself and my surrounding, continues with this poetry book, which is my third. Yet this book has an updated, more mature less innocent, perspective regarding love, hatred, life, death, faith and trust.

As the book is a collection of poems, I had many emotional states while writing it. In fact, those emotional states are the true authors, and poets. Most of the poems are directly inspired by my everyday happenings, yet dive deep into the eternal nature of the human in us.

A Heartbeat at Arles

I remember those streets,
The night was growing thin,
I heard your heartbeats,
I felt your blazing skin,
We sat on that terrace,
We both did fight and win,
You held my hand in fear,
You spoke with so much pain,
When tomorrow is right here
And sun is out again,
Will you still call me dear?
Will you still love me then?

That night, that gorgeous blue,
Those lights of divinity,
The skies, they looked so new,
Your eyes were sanity,
I lay there next to you,
We mocked our vanity,
You asked me with a tear,
That your heart did drain,
When tomorrow is right here,
And sun is out again,
Will you still call me dear?
Will you still love me then?

Then after the night grew ill,
And we quenched our thirst,
A breaking light did spill,
That dawn was our first,
I watched your sleep until,
You woke up at will,

You saw me still near,
You looked at me with sheer,
Tomorrow is right here,
And sun is out again,
I'm still calling you dear,
I'm still loving you then.

Sonnet 31

Preface

This sonnet is a divine conversation and an analytical approach to pain.

As a child, I surely enjoyed and laughed many hours per day, yet I also spent many hours at night, crying in the comfort of my parents.

As a teenager, I cried when I lost my father to sudden death, then as an adult, I cried upon the loss of my sister to illness.

Life, as generous and as happy as it can be, can undoubtedly be painful and bitter as well.

When I see a bee in spring, and ponder the short lifespan of bees and the vivacity of their movements, I think of life and death, how they are strongly interconnected, and how through their contrast, joy and pain make us smile and cry.

Sonnet 31

An infant I cried when my cradle shook,
By the wind which from the unknown did blow,
And down to the earth, to my room it took,
My sleep and left me full of night and awe.
A teenage I cried when the thirsty death,
Drank from my abundant generous well,
And out of my happy lungs, a dear breath,
Elapsed in silence, unable to tell.
An adult I cried when I lost a face,
In a robbery that the passing days,
Had committed against my heedless pace,
As if they took from the noon sun its rays.
When a spring bee I see, I think of Thee,
I gaze at life, and death gazes back at me.

Pestilence

Around the pillars of justice,
Power has married greed,
And their children, ever since,
Have been playing around,
With dynamite and fire.

Sonnet 32

Preface

This sonnet is again a divine conversation, this time analysing the damage of excessive pleasure.
The instant gratification of the world we live in, has led many, including myself, to lose much of their time and possessions.
The wealth of a sound mind and body can easily be lost through incontinent lust and ecstasy.
Thus, a desert of abundant delights may lead to a parching thirst, as the desertification of one's own world turns out to be a personal choice, whether intentional or not.

Sonnet 32

In a desert of distraction and joy,
I lose my long-borne wealth of lofty thoughts,
I roam a clearing in which pleasures cloy,
Coming from open ecstasy-filled spots.
In a river which from delight is dry,
I lose a murmuring crystalline brook,
A running clarity of studies high,
Encompassing the power of a book.
In a gloomy, poorly lit cobwebbed room,
Where still is the air, and hefty the dust,
I lose a dawning beam touching a bloom,
Of a wild young rose triumphing with lust.
Many goods I lose in dead sites for sure,
But in Thee shall I seek and find the cure.

My Bonds of Freedom

I stood upon the shoulder of Qadisha Valley
And gazed downwards, to where the river
Serpented in serene secludedness, with waters,
Murmuring and hugging dearly my heartbeats,
And the rocks of the vale sang a lullaby
Of exceeding tenderness to my soul.
Day after day, bonds of longing
And of love, were born and strengthened,
As roots, between the valley and me.
Until one day, I couldn't tarry longer,
For change had called me, so I had to move
And leave behind the valley I loved.
I left those murmurs sweet, those songs tender.
Hence the bonds of longing and of love
Were weakened, then cut altogether.
Days went heedlessly fast, until one evening,

An unusual wind blew against my senses,
It exploded a rebellious soul in my sails
And filled my vessels with ambitious flames.
Day after day, bonds of longing
And of love, were born and strengthened,
As winter storms, between the wind and me.
Until one day, the wind couldn't tarry longer,
For horizon had called it, and it had to move,
And leave me behind, so I remained
Unable to catch the speedy forsaking wind.
Hence the bonds of longing, and of love
Were weakened, then cut altogether.
Here I am, passing by, and standing, once again
Upon the shoulder of the sacred Qadisha Valley
Once again, the waters of Qadisha River are hugging
My heartbeats and the rocks are singing to my soul
The same old lullaby, which is now even much sweeter,
And my senses yield flowers of virgin fire.

While I stand, with wandering thoughts and still steps
And out of the heavy surrounding trees and bushes,
A well-known wind blew against my senses
Against my sails, again, and again against my vessels
And a rebellious soul, along with ambitious flames
Dance in the space of my presence.
Here I stand, a wiser man, upon wisdom itself,
Gazing with mortal senses, at immortality.
I close my eyes, and smile with sweet bitterness,
If I shall die, this is where I wish to,
Unto the rhythm of blowing winds and flowing waters.
I open then my eyes, turn my back to the vale, and leave,
Free of bonds, full of passion and love.

Sonnet 33

Preface

We always desire to have what can soothe our annoyances, and we get creative in fashioning the best artificial atmosphere not to disturb our joy.

We long for warm places in cold winters,

And find ourselves drawn to cool ones in summer, for extreme temperatures make us uncomfortable and sick.

We also long for our beloved ones,

And even when pleasures are all around us, we still miss that which can ignite in us a sense of existence and belonging.

Sonnet 33

I long for a breeze which is somehow cool,
In the dead stillness of hot summer days,
To soothe the burning heat of sun so cruel,
From which descends the deadly healing rays.
I long for a breeze which is somehow warm,
In the freezing young lively winter wind,
To soothe the bone-chilling blasting storm,
That ice inflicts upon me as a fiend.
I long for a breath coming from your lips,
In the garden of pleasure when I walk,
As if in my mouth, your bonny taste drips,
As if I conceal your name when I talk.
Tell me how, when my eyes wander and blink,
You explode in my thoughts and in my ink.

Inner Sight

The power of an eye is killed by doubt.
Silence is a higher communication.
The shades of beauty are everywhere.
A soul in pain is a caged eagle.
An eye is a mirror of the soul.

Sonnet 34

Preface

In a reality that lacks a simple logical structure, one cannot but question the application of Justice.

What can justify the fault of a rich man and condemn the same fault of a poor one?

And why some humans are allowed to break the rules while others are strictly punished?

Is Justice really a virtue? Or a sociological invention to protect those who invented it from the other group of people?

Here I express my torture of thought when it comes to realising corruption, which is one of the main faces of injustice.

Sonnet 34

A trace I trace, with a hasty lively pace,
A thread of sanity, so I shall find,
A truth, a word, a proof, maybe a face,
Or what can put to rest my lusty mind.
A mould I mould in which I try to see,
What flies above the clouds of desire,
Justice is no longer great and free,
As if its pillars are set on fire.
A write I write as if I seek and look,
Between my own lines for what can lead me,
To the secret I dropped in my own book,
And sealed it with a lock, then lost the key.
I wonder if, one day, the Truth I meet,
Will I be the first to perceive and greet?

Natural Selection

It was dusk, and the sky was dim,
Fog started to dilate slow,
Upon the northern forest rim,
Hunting sights, in blinding woe.

Through the fog, a heedful pace,
Cracked the stems of wood,
A hunter had left his place,
To come back with some food.

There would wait until he's back,
His two children alone,
Believing in their father's knack,
To end their hungry moan.

Yet another hunter was there,
Among the half-seen trees,
With brown fur and wilderness fair,
She was smelling the breeze.

A grizzly mother with two cubs,
Had been starving all day,
She smelled across the dense shrubs,
A prey and came all the way.

A caring soul charged a caring soul,
An empty core crashed an empty core,
Wild aggression was released whole,
And human blood stained the timber floor.

Sonnet 35

Preface

Memories make us question the reality of our feelings, connections, and certainty.

The more distant they are, the more prone to be distorted, raising doubt about anything, anyone, and any former state of mind.

In the complexion of thoughts, about Truth and Life, we encounter simple situations which easily draw us out from the turmoil of thinking, into a simplified state of beauty and satisfaction.

In a literary abstraction, I write this sonnet, and I highly value the beauty of nature and its instant effect on our understanding and state of mind.

Sonnet 35

Into a maze of memories, I tread,
With half faces, half stories, and half names,
As if the days when I smiled and I bled,
Together they merged and shared all their flames.
Into a vale of half-seen end I sink,
I tumble down and I fall with great speed,
Towards the vicissitude when I think,
Of truth that consumes all my thought and heed.
Into an ocean of bottomless shade,
I dive with heavy body and scarce breath,
To seek life when my breathing starts to fade,
And my numb senses are approaching death.
In a morning, when birds sing merrily,
I witness life, and life does sing to me.

The Buried Hope

Once again, a nursing mother seeks the scattered pieces of the cradle, tinted with blood, bearing a dying limb, on a dying body.

Once again, the resting workers are blasted, and the good they built with their good hearts, is being devoured by the evil of those whose hearts beat with evil.

Once again, I put my hand on a wound that is bleeding, and out of its pain, a loud voice emerges and calls upon another beloved bleeding wound.

Once again, the shepherds lead the wolves into the hangar at night, where their own sheep are vulnerably sleeping.

Once again, the lamenting loss visits our streets, shaking the pillars of half-stable years and sowing destructive chaos, hopelessness, death, and rage.

Nay, this time is different!

It is greater than all times.

The nursing mother has found naught but a part of her own, kissed by ugliness in a mere calamity. And a wail is trembling the half-standing room.

The workers are no more but a screaming memory, sweet yet bitter to the unforgetting senses in the hearts of their beloved.

The wound beneath my hand is still bleeding now with blood and tears, yet, it has stopped calling! For now, we both know that the other wound has stopped bleeding, and turned cold, and white.

The shepherds have put on their wolf-like masks, and followed the wolves into the hangar. They have witnessed the massacre, and now are sharing the flesh of all their own slain sheep.

This time, the scent of blood that loss has spread is surpassed by the scent of corruption.

There was a field, much rich, much envied.

The protectors of that field got hungry for gold, forgetting that their honour and their roots were within the field they were trusted to defend.

They had got their gold, and set free the rats into the harvest, eating, ruining, and leaving a devastated yield.

But the protectors of the field got hungry again, and they got more gold, and set fire to what was left, turning it into barren land.

And again, the insatiable greed got more and more gold and piled upon the barren burnt field and under its ground, a pestilence, and a curse.

Now the bleached fresh bones of dead children and the weeping of the cut flesh, are echoes that will never cease to disrupt the wicked souls who sold their own priceless parents and children.

Lebanon,

The ever-envied field,

The dawn of literature as we know it, the dwelling of the First Written Alphabet.

The rich shore hugged by the sun, the dwelling of the legendary Imperial Purple Murex.

The lofty mountain secluded into clouds of lofty air, the dwelling of the Cedars of God.

Lebanon,

How oft, oh how oft, had you fallen, and burnt.

And how oft, oh how oft had you risen again from between your own ashes.

How oft, oh how oft the legendary Phoenix has burnt through your men and women, whose brains are sanctuaries of wisdom, whose hearts are wells of fondness, whose souls are fearless, and bodies are weapons of justice.

To the majority of our dear leaders

Who sold our country as a foreign piece of land, to foreign people

And chose the gold in their pockets upon the dignity of their people.

You do not deserve to be called Lebanese.

The scent of your corruption is much foul

And it offends my senses.

And your deals of ugliness
Are plain obvious and plainly ugly.
You are not Lebanon,
You are but a sick phase of our country.
Hoping soon that it will recover
From your illness
And the Phoenix will again
Ignite with righteousness
Over the ashes
With flames burning the wicked
And lighting again upon the dark, barren field,
Reviving the Buried Hope.

Sonnet 36

Preface

Sometimes, we witness a shift in the behaviour of a person, or in our own behaviour. And that shift makes us think about what has happened and induced that change.

From stagnation and demotivation, to the phases of growth, then back to the circle of self-questioning, the journey of exploring one's own self is a tough one, yet much fruitful.

In this sonnet, I am pondering the change which left me at my lowest points and thinking of the many contrasts and contradictions that people teach regarding this issue.

When I look into an analogue clock, the hands go up till twelve, and then go down again.

They resemble some birds rooted in a way which allows them to fly, yet reminds them always of their origin, so they do not fly away, but keep circling the same place.

Sonnet 36

They say one must grow and never be still,
For stillness is but a poisoning fiend,
That with ease can intoxicate and kill,
And leave a blank future, empty and cleaned.
They say to grow; one must look at the sky,
Towards sun, one must leave behind the ground,
Above the past, one has to soar and fly,
From earth to be free, to heavens be bound.
But they say the higher you throw a rock,
The more hastily it tumbles and falls,
Just as the hour hand of the same clock,
Which hits the twelve, when noon or midnight calls.
Your memory lifts me up to the highs,
Your reality drags me down with cries.

My Homeland

(Written in Terza Rima)

A silent breeze I woke and flew
Upon my beloved homeland
With a heart filled with darkish blue

I saw virtues had turned to sand
And the malignant had taken charge
With a greedy hungry hand

People's hope had lost the marge
And the child had died in the womb
Of a pregnant of no discharge

A breeze I went and saw the doom
A raging tempest I came back
To avenge the innocent womb

Sonnet 37

Preface

Following the bad news of racism around the globe, especially the story of Georges Perry Floyd, I write this piece to emphasise the idea of true value.

My eyes are important to take convenient decisions, yet in some scenarios, one should really pay attention to the third eye, and sense what is beyond colours and shapes.

In a world, where skin colour is interfering with the value of a human being, it is such a sad reality to acknowledge how far we are from living the concept of humanity.

Sonnet 37

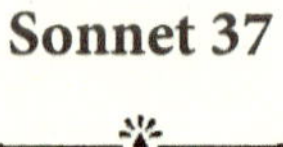

How dear are the blackish hours when by,
A beautiful soul I pass at dark night,
So clear is the judgement of the third eye,
When free of misleading faces and light.
How dear are the bright hours of the day,
In which I deem what my vision adores,
To keep what might inflict the pain at bay,
To shut the wrong, and open the right doors.
To deem my heart, to deem my soul and aim,
Is to know me much, to explore my well,
The fact that I'm right or wrong, strong or lame,
Is beyond what my skin colour can tell.
How I ponder with much love and delight,
The words of writers, whether black or white.

In Mid of My Grieves (Haiku)

In mid of my grieves
I beheld my higher self
I smiled in silence

I smiled in silence
When I learned how to accept
The lot of my self

The lot of my self
Was shown by my higher self
In mid of my grieves

Sonnet 38

Preface

There are times when we get hit by memories,
Memories of those are no more.

Times when a beloved face flashes before our eyes,
and feels so real.

Times when we relive the pain and the joy of the past
in a daydreaming trance.

Times when all we want is to just wander in thought,
and beat at heart.

Sonnet 38

At times I sit, within myself I look,
My joy and pain, my sun and rain, I see,
As if my years are pages in a book,
Well-sealed, yet I set all the pages free!
At times, your lofty thoughts and dreamy face,
Flash back as stormy waves and crash on me,
As if I'm a shore for the yore to chase,
And scatter my past in my future sea.
At times you cross, as a warm yellow ray,
My icy winter, burdened with dark clouds,
As if a pure child who just wants to play,
Is passing through demonic villain crowds.
How oft I sit, with a wandering mind,
When your memories seek my heed, and find.

As if I'm Still with You

I wonder how are you,
Where all is dark and blue,
I wonder if you knew,
I would always miss you,
As if you're still around,
As if I'm still with you.

I know I have no choice,
I always hear your voice,
Perhaps it isn't you,
Perhaps it's something new,
As if you're still around,
As if I'm still with you.

Tomorrow when the rain,
Will hit the streets again,
I'll walk again with you
We'll talk and we'll laugh too,
As if you're still around,
As if I'm still with you.
I sleep and stretch my arm,
To hug again your charm,
But oh, my darling though,
You travelled to the blue,
I live as if you're here,
As if I'm still with you.

Sonnet 39

Preface

This is an interpretation of a spiritual journey
from dawn to dusk.

Through which we find ourselves consoled and
comforted by a belief, a person, an ideology,
or even a memory.

Dawn, being the birth of a human,

It is, for sure, adorned with innocence and growth.

Noon is the mid-age, when lust and greed grow wild,

And pollute a major part of the initial innocence.

Dusk is the final phase, often described as wise.

In this phase, the idea of mortality is prominent,

And the strength of a human shifts to its true form.

Sonnet 39

I smiled when the thick darkness of my own,
Began to languish before my young eyes,
I did burst then throughout my lovely dawn,
And sent my keen innocence to the skies.
Until at noon, I lost my heed somewhere,
Between my lust and my sparkling dust,
The hasty dusk hit my note unaware,
Hence I saw, in choking awe, my dim crust.
A flowering Grand Duke of Tuscany,
You fairly stood on my darkening soil,
Oh, what remedy, to my eyes and me,
What consoling oil, to my tough turmoil.
How deceitful our mind, when we rejoice,
Yet my peace I find, in your scent and voice.

Sonnet 40

Preface

The balance,
The symbol that stands upon courts,
The protector of rights,
Justice.

I gaze through the wilderness, and I see the weakest deer killed by the tiger, so that the tiger may live. Then I see the strongest deer escape a tiger, so that the deer may live.

Then I rejoice sun and wind, which hug with gifts both tigers and deer.

Then again, I turn my face to the streets, and see the wealthy enacting laws to protect themselves from the poor. And the rights of those who lack gold are often murdered naked in front of the public, shamelessly.

I then bless the honesty and the purity of wilderness, and I write.

Sonnet 40

In the dead of night, the woods shook with fright,
And death befell to give more days of life,
The weakest was killed after a short fight,
And the strongest lived for another strife.
The night has gone, and now the morning dew,
Sparkles upon, flowers and grass and trees,
Upon them all shines the same day anew,
With the same sun, and blows the very breeze.
Then at times of gloom, when days become cold,
The fox and the hare, their game remains fair,
None of them is poor, none of them has gold,
They drink the same water, and breathe the same air.
Justice full of lies, in the streets I see,
Yet in the dear wild, it's all honesty.

A Second Chance

What if;

One night you sit,

In your dark pit,

You start to get hit,

Pain keeps hitting you

With shit, so that you shall quit.

What if;

Your dreams that night,

Start to die, no light,

In your head, you get blues instead,

Around your head, your thoughts fight,

From your brain, they eat,

Bite by bite until,

Inside you, they ignite,

Black fire, you know,

That isn't right,

What if;
The mistake you did,
Has blown you away,
The way you think is hidden,
Your wishes are,
Like a dying star, amid,
Your wishes dance,
The devil's kid,
That you can't forbid,
What if;
The night is dark, and dark
Are your thoughts, that bark,
Within your heart,
They start,
To rip you apart, you know,
From now nothing can grow
In your garden,
Full of dark snow.

What if;

The next day you live in a trance,

And suddenly, you get a glance

Of purity, sweet reality,

You have a second chance,

What if, you have a second chance,

To live again, no pain,

To dance, to plan in advance,

How will you take it,

What will be your stance?

What if;

Your life spins around,

The hope you lost and found,

Now you, you live like new,

In a world that is more true,

Only a few got that new,

Second chance you're getting

The key, you can see,

Is in never forgetting

That lesson taught,

To you and me.

What if;

Sonnet 41

Preface

How oft a memory of a beloved one, can be so true that one may doubt that death really occurred.

How oft we hold dear, even the traces of yesterday, in things and places and hours, hoping to regain what is irreversibly lost.

And how, in front of the sea, I gaze at waves, as they look like people, being born, growing, then decaying with foam and falling, then disappearing.

And I write the memory and the present.

Sonnet 41

Losing my heed after your sight and smell,
Around your locks rustles my eager breath,
The shades of our pleasures are my sweet hell,
Nay you do not seem encircled by death.
At times when you come across me, I think,
Of the foe in the tricky passing days,
You ignite my senses, and through my ink,
You burst with life again in many ways.
As a seed you come, and I hold you dear,
Into my rich soil with exceeding care,
Every time that you may grow and stay near,
Yet oh, each time you leave my soil so bare.
I ponder, when before the raging sea,
The rising and falling waves I do see.

Sweet Turbulence

(Elfchen chain)

Beauty,
The misunderstood,
The partially hidden,
The sacred sublime secret,
Divine,
Silent upon,
The closed lip,
Desire's hot impatient flames,
Passion,
Increasingly built,
Illogical yet true,
Unstoppable yet so fragile,
Beauty,

Sonnet 42

Preface

I sit betwixt my failure and my success; I weigh them both and put them into the scale of giving.

An abundance, which is grown in talkative and chaos, yet it can only be reaped in silence and in the low tide of mind.

As I see the scale is no more even, I ponder in astonishment.

Sonnet 42

I looked upon the field which stood at right,
Where I sowed years back half of my dear seeds,
I saw there that the hopes and deeds were right,
And I smiled with all my satisfied needs.
Then I looked upon the field at my left,
Where I sowed the other half of my dear seeds,
And I saw a bare land, with nothing left,
But a rotten foul soil and few sick weeds.
In rage I thought of what I could have brought,
With me when at left, I left my young hope,
My little mind grew with what my heed caught,
Around my dying seeds that could not cope.
My success gave me much, yet more I care
Of what my failure with me does share.

The Ease in Storms (Haiku)

When Luck goes forlorn,

And Doubt is uglily born,

Accept! And hold on.

Sonnet 43

Preface

I believe death and love,
Have turned us all into poets.
When I think of, how a face,
Or a place, or a phrase, can set our minds
Into fire, an unrestrained one,
Blazing our hearts too.
And how we know that we are vulnerable
Before these faces and places and phrases.
With all our thoughts and heartbeats
That will no longer stay ours,
But flow chainless, with a self-willingness.

Sonnet 43

I sat on the warm countless grains of sand,
I turned my back to the limitless blue,
Then took a part of the beach in my hand,
And loosed my fingers to let it slip through.
The falling grains of yellow were windblown,
And got scattered, some near, some far away
As if they sought to go each on their own,
And I gave them the chance, and showed the way.
Then I turned my face to the restless sea,
And as the grains of sand, my thoughts slipped out,
Scattered, never willing to stay with me,
Dissolving my heart in a foam of rout.
Tell me how, my quick thoughts can I withhold,
When freedom in your face do I behold?

September Breeze

I wake up to my routine day,
On an autumn's morning grey,
I look out to behold the skies,
Up there, I see your tender eyes,
Oh, darling, then you come to me,
And we sit on our balcony.
What else my heart always seeks,
But the spring within your cheeks?
My day with me you come and spend,
Yet no one knows since I pretend,
That you are no longer around,
But only in death can be found,
And when the evening comes again,

To our balcony, we go, and then,
Our dreams of youth we hunt and chase,
With the spring blooming your face.
I reach the night to sleep with ease,
How can I, with this heavy breeze?!
September comes, September goes,
In my garden, your flower grows,
Oh, darling, then you come to me,
You enter my dreams merrily,
I live the spring in autumn though,
I will be sleeping without you.

Sonnet 44

Preface

Reading through the writing of a friend,
THE BURDEN OF BEING HUMAN
Raising the question of true morality,
And its arbitrary aspect.
I, too, am searching for Truth.
We often search too far,
Before returning to the very place
We always used to dwell in.
Only to find there
What we couldn't find everywhere else.
And the bird of Light,
That we cannot find in the forests of the world;
Is waiting for us in the single tree near our home.
I think of Truth again, and I write.

Sonnet 44

I hunted Truth down the valleys of lies,
Around my neck, I hung its holy name,
On the steep roads, I confronted the wise,
Along with the fool, the swift, and the lame.
I've been execrated for seeking Light,
In the low recesses of a dark vale,
As if through the hooting owls of the night,
One was seeking a singing nightingale!
Between the arbitrary moral laws,
Too many reflections turned my eyes blind,
Until a moment of peace without flaws,
Towards nature diverted my limp mind.
As I changed my view for Truth's divine sake,
Amid darkness, I saw the Light awake.

Autumn Breeze

Oh, autumn breeze, of tender joy,
How can you be so glad?
As if sadness is but a toy,
And nothing can be bad.
Oh, autumn breeze, tell me how,
Your placid, serene heart,
With so much peace is kissing now,
The leaves to fall apart?

Would you please sing for me,
Your joyous lullaby?
Sing for me
Your secret song
How can you be
So strong?

You know the leaves are green,
Full of colour and life,
All summer, they have been,
So abundant and rife,
And here you come to kiss,
The green with your smile,
You greet the trees with bliss,
Yet you carry a guile.

Now would you sing for me,
Your joyous lullaby?
Sing for me
Your secret song
How can you be
So strong?

Oh, autumn breeze, I envy you,
You are the starter of cold,
Winter is in the heart of you,
But you never let it unfold,
Never harsh, always tender,
Until the green is yellow,
Until the calm surrender.
Until the silent sparrow.

Now would you sing for me
Your joyous lullaby?
Sing for me
Whether right or wrong!
How can you be
So strong?

Sonnet 45

Preface

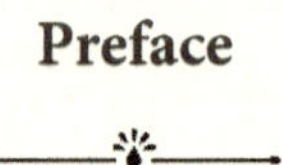

When virtue and vice get into conflict
within a human,

The search for truth prevails,
and the journey of wisdom starts.

How often do we abstain from some activities,
To eventually come back and break the pre-set rules.

How often do we re-evaluate our definitions,
And we recalculate our aims, our needs,

To end up turning the tables on the old,
embracing the new.

Sonnet 45

I thought the days of vice would never come,
My senses loathed sin and kept it at bay,
Yet a pleasurable rhythm of a drum,
Left in my ear a lusty wicked play.
How oft in my proud and luxurious trance,
I did long for pleasure, but acted not,
How true was Blake's claim, for I made a lance,
That pierced my core with a satanic shot.
At death I gaze, through death I clearly see,
What life teaches and yields, preaches and writes,
At sin I gaze, through sin I find the key
To the masked virtues in turbulent nights.
In a solitude of thought, I behold,
The divine iron, and the nasty gold.

Inner Faith (Haiku)

In churches and mosques,
Many do not find the peace,
Offered by Nature.

Sonnet 46

Preface

I sit near a fire and watch the flies of the night,
Coming again and again,
To end up being burnt and dead.
I think of the peace they are trying to get, unwavering.
And then I look to our society,
And to the crimes we commit in the name of peace.
Are we committing suicide?
The way those flies are killing themselves unaware?
Then I take a pen, and I write.

Sonnet 46

Nigh a campfire, on a chill black night,
I see dead and limping flies on the ground,
They neared to seek the warmth, to seek the light,
Yet, in their own understanding were drowned.
No peace was there in the vacuous dark,
Neither here upon the flames of fire,
Unless in death and death is the hallmark,
Of peace, then let us in death aspire.
Upon my people, I cast a sad look,
For in the name of Peace, we rape and kill,
Then we fake Truth and put it in a book,
To cover our ill, and the blood we spill.
In the wilderness, I search and I find,
Much more peace than in the realm of mankind.

Satisfaction

(Elfchen Chain)

Hunger,
Residing over,
My rooted desires,
Calling the filthy pleasure,
Impatiently,
Humming through,
The vales of,
Imminent sins and transgressions,
Naked,
Outlaw desires,
Through heavy chains,
And tight thick ropes,
Brutally,
And instantly,
Relieving my desires,
From their and my,
Hunger.

Sonnet 47

Preface

The will to overtake,

To overpower,

To rule,

The misunderstanding of spirituality,

The altered sense of wisdom,

The bloodshed,

The flames,

The rape,

The massacres,

All beneath the mask of skin colour
and religious backgrounds!

Sonnet 47

I gave the guardians of my saneness,
A recess to lay their burdens aside,
And I tossed the fears that fed my lameness,
Off the cliffs of my magnitude and pride.
Saneness is conditioned by where I live,
Hence, I soar and hover above the earth,
And drop my thoughts which with warm love I give,
To rain o'er the black and white with much mirth.
Whether born on the calm Tibetan hills,
Or through the Arabian blazing sand,
Or upon the ranging Alps full of chills,
Slaying each other must come to an end.
Through the bloody deeds of religious rage,
Flow the sad tears of the kind-hearted sage.

The Bohemian Bar

Alone, alone, as if unknown,
At the Bohemian bar I sat,
I drank and drank until the tone
Of music was almost gone,
Under my silly hat.
Midnight passed me by,
As if I was a stone,
My head was low,
My glass was high,
There she came to say hi.
Let's drink a glass or two,
For a fresh and new start,
She said and smiled at me,
And I was drunk at heart.

We were two waves at shore,
Breaking before we die,
We drank a little more,
We laughed; she and I,
We drank until the dawn,
Was already there,
And the heed of my own,
Had left me unaware.
Let's go out, you and me,
For a fresh and new start,
She said and smiled at me,
And I was drunk at heart.

We could barely walk,
In Beirut, cool morn,
But we continued to talk,
Until the sun was born,
Until the sun's warm rays,
Scattered her face apart,
Until she turned to haze,
In the memory of my heart,
Oh yes, we spent the night,
Even if we were apart,
Alone, and that's alright,
For I was drunk at heart.

Sonnet 48

Preface

In the cold breeze of autumn, where death and life wrestle, I think of divinity.

In a thought regarding Saints,

And how their names are upon restaurants, pharmacies, cities.

We use those names in ignorance of what they bear, and of the culture behind them.

Sonnet 48

We are heedless when we utter your names,
And your names are in almost every place,
We are heedful when we pursue our aims,
And our aims may kill us at every pace.
On a flying wing, I ponder your thought,
And stretch your depths into the heights of skies,
Where your superhuman souls rest and float,
Free of deceitful acts and free of lies.
Around your perfect lines cries the calm mirth,
And joyfully basks with rot far under,
As if the restless ever spinning earth,
Has found a place to rest and wonder.
In an autumn breeze, I smell Death, and I,
Gaze at vernal Life with my inner eye.

My Falling Leaf (Haiku)

I asked the autumn
Where is my love? It sent me
A dead falling leaf

Sonnet 49

Preface

Sometimes, it is the closest person to us who
inflicts the most devastating damage.

Sometimes, the problem lies in the trust
we blindly give.

Some people with outer beauty,
are full of inner ugliness,

And through the journey of life, we get to know better,

How to steer away from human toxicity,

Hence, we may well find peace with lesser company,

Or even with none at all.

Sonnet 49

I thought some people I knew were pillars,
Upon which my future time would take place,
Until the day they turned to be killers,
Murderers of trust, murderers of pace.
They arrayed their mansions with the bright days,
On their balconies, flowers full of life,
Yet behind their walls, their mean foul ways
Gave birth to a wicked death-bearing knife.
Out of their bewitching houses, in fear,
I ran and gathered myself in my dink,
Away from the fraudulent, I did steer,
Through the river of dignity and ink.
In my lonely times, I search and I seek,
Then I find the wisdom of which I speak.

A Betrayal (Haiku)

I saw a weird sheep,
With a wolf mask neath its fleece,
Sheep's blood on its hooves.

Sonnet 50

Preface

How oft we travel to the ancient era in us.

To the time when we were immensely growing and immensely learning.

To where beauty still lives, undisturbed in our thoughts, and purity unwavering.

How oft, we seek peace there, and then we travel back to the present, with an inner serenity.

Sonnet 50

Oh, what mirth, what serenity and peace,
When I backwardly cast a gazing look,
At the sea where all turbulent thoughts cease,
And memories murmur as a calm brook.
Oh, what calmness my disturbed soul does feel,
When upon the blue of the past I roam,
And all my wounds seem to blossom and heal,
When my sight rejoices through the white foam.
And all of a sudden, I travel back,
To the present beat, to the present breath,
To witness my mind dressed up in full black,
At the funeral of my bright past death.
A smile when no other eyes are to see,
Is an insight grasped out of that blue sea.

Covid Days

I sit alone,
No place to go,
The fun is gone,
The mood so low,
My coffee black,
I do prepare,
Will they come back
My nights so fair?
How much I hate,
These days too sad,
As if my fate,
Is going mad,
I often stand,
On balcony,
Within my hand,

There stands with me,
My coffee black,
No milk, no sweet,
My eyes do track,
The empty street,
How much I hate,
These days too sad,
As if my fate
Is going mad.
There passed by,
A lady fair,
She looked up high,
With golden hair,
That dog she walked,
Was pretty small,
Her feet he stalked,
And chased her call,

She put on no mask,
She walked untamed,
I had to ask,
About her name!
My coffee black,
I left when she,
Slowed down and back,
She smiled at me,
Went down to her,
With my request,
With her small dog,
Would be my guest,
Forgot about,
Covid-19,
When I saw out,

That pretty scene,
Since then, we sit,
And laugh and talk,
No mask we fit,
We walk the dog,
My coffee black,
Still I prepare,
Now they are back,
My nights so fair,
How much I love,
These days too mad!
We never know,
When we'll be glad.

The Will of Poseidon

Preface

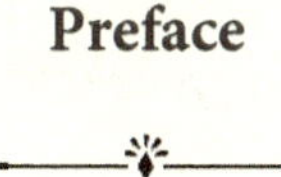

This is a tribute to the Lebanese painter Najwa Nahas, who lost her father to the sea when she was but a child. The poem is based on a painting by the artist, where a memory of a seascape sends her right back to her childhood every time.

The Will of Poseidon

Thirteen years unaware,
Of what might you be,
Of your full love and care,
Of whom you were to me,
And then, with burst unfair,
You left me for the sea.

That boat I steer and sail,
As if your hand with mine,
Whether in sun or hail,
To be my lifeline,
So, I will never fail,
And all will be fine.

You left as fading wave,
And each time I do stand,
At Tripoli's shore, I wave,
With my heart's fond hand,
To your secluded grave,
Beneath sea ribbed sand.

In every time my thought,
My passing hours surmount
I bless that Mina's coast,
In a trance I lose count,
Of the years on that boat,
In front of Terbol Mount.

And then the trident spoke,
And my deep skills awoke,
And I painted my memory,
With unrestrained stroke,
Poseidon's will made me cry,
Made me doubt and ask why,
Made me burn with colours,
And yield an eternal eye.

About the Poet

Ziad Jreige is a versatile artist and poet, born in Kousba, Lebanon 1986. He obtained his Nursing degree from the Lebanese University in 2008, then pursued various courses in English Literature and painting, broadening his artistic and literary practice.

Jreige's work delves into the human experience, exploring themes ranging from pain and anxiety to pleasure and faith. His expression is vastly inspired by the mountainous landscapes of his childhood and the frequent exposure to human vulnerability through his nursing profession. Influenced by his father, an Arabic teacher and literature enthusiast, as well as by notable figures like Gibran Kahlil Gibran, William Blake, and The Romantics. He entwines together the familiar and the well-known with the philosophy of scepticism and spiritual satisfaction.

As an accomplished poet, Jreige has published three poetry books, showcasing his unique perspective and poetic voice.

Also by Ziad

The Nightingale: His Poems and Paintings of Dawn

The King of Rimes

www.ingramcontent.com/pod-product-compliance
Lightning Source LLC
La Vergne TN
LVHW091034150826
845672LV00006BA/1801